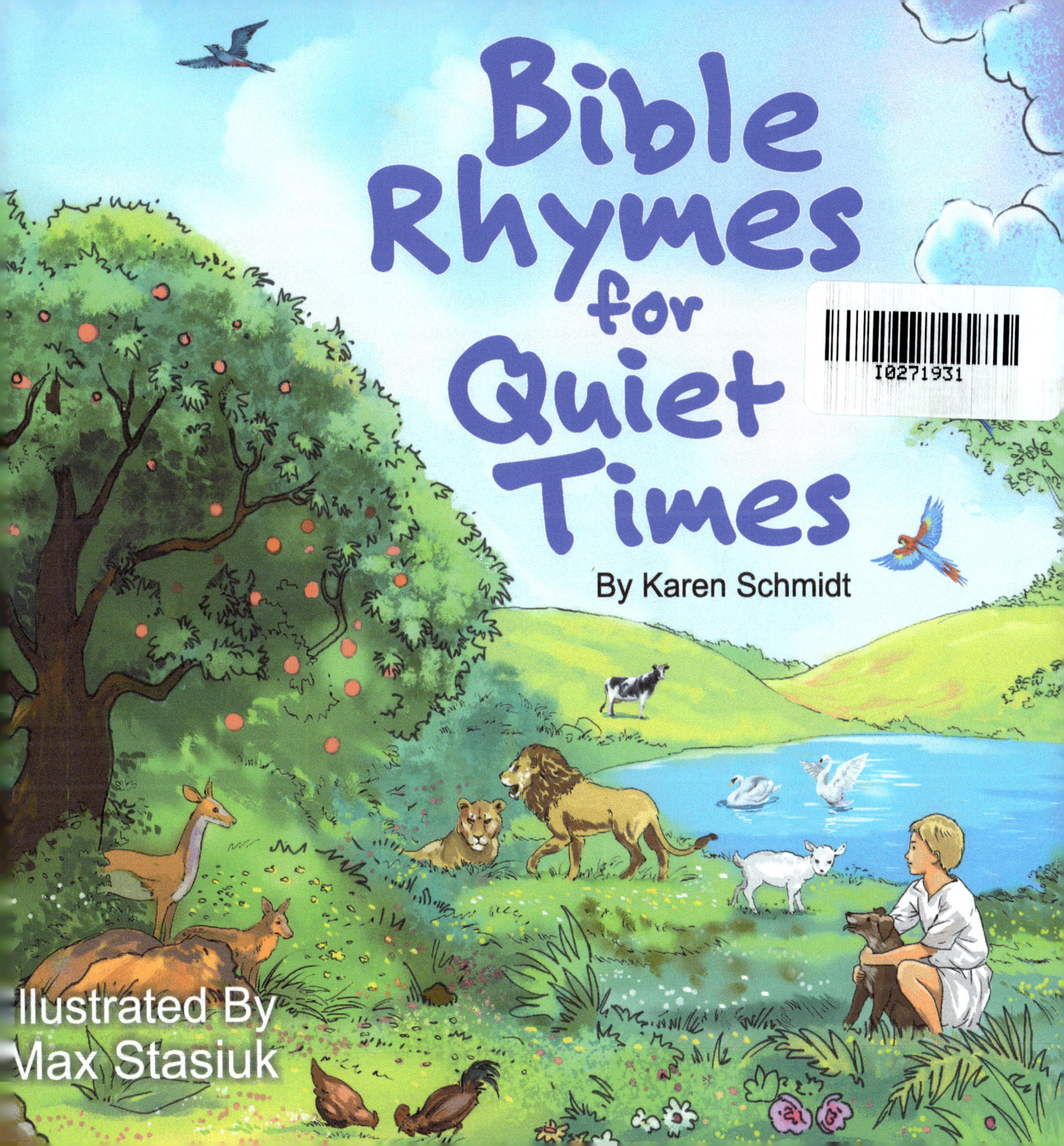

World rights reserved. This book or any portion thereof may not be copied or reproduced in any form or manner whatever, except as provided by law, without the written permission of the publisher, except by a reviewer who may quote brief passages in a review.

The author assumes full responsibility for the accuracy of all facts and quotations as cited in this book. The opinions expressed in this book are the author's personal views and interpretations, and do not necessarily reflect those of the publisher.

This book is provided with the understanding that the publisher is not engaged in giving spiritual, legal, medical, or other professional advice. If authoritative advice is needed, the reader should seek the counsel of a competent professional.

Copyright © 2017 Karen Schmidt

Copyright © 2017 TEACH Services, Inc.

ISBN-13: 978-1-4796-0710-5 (Paperback)

ISBN-13: 978-1-4796-0711-2 (ePub)

ISBN-13: 978-1-4796-0712-9 (Mobi)

Library of Congress Control Number: 2016920139

Scripture quotations marked KJV are taken from the King James Version.

Table of Contents

God's Letter 4
Light Your Candle 5
Eden Lost 6
The Ark 8
Jacob's Lie 10
Holy Spirit 11
King Saul 12
Basket Boat 13
Jehoshaphat 14
God's Home 16
The Widow's Mite 17
Building a Temple 18
Mary, Mary 19
The Lion's Den 20
Peter Goes Free 21
Eutychus 22
Lost and Found 24
Black Sheep 25
Jesus and Lucifer 26
Three Angels 28
Bible Texts & Thoughts For Parents 32

GOD'S LETTER

God wrote
A letter to me
On two tables of stone.

Now it's written
In my heart
To share with everyone.

LIGHT YOUR CANDLE

Light your candle,

Hold it high

For all the world to see.

When God looks down

He'll see your light,

Say, "You belong to me."

EDEN LOST

Adam,
The man
Made of clay,
Sat up
And looked
All around
Him in awe.

Then
As a gift
To Adam,
God gave
Him the world
That he saw.

Adam knew
At that moment
How rich
He would be,
But gave
It away……
 At the forbidden tree.

THE ARK

The unclean
Came by twos,
The clean ones
Came by sevens.
When all the
Animals
Had come inside,
God opened up
The heavens.

Pitter, Patter, Pit,
The drops began to fall.
Noah heard them as they hit,
They were very small.

Split, Splat, Splatter,
The rain came falling down,
But it didn't matter,
All were safe and sound.

JACOB'S LIE

Jacob told a lie
And ran away,
But God still
Loved him anyway.

Jacob's ladder,
Tall and straight,
Reaches up
To heaven's gate.

Angels come
From heaven bright
To safely guard me
Through the night.

Jacob fought the angel,
Won at last,
Forgiveness for
His lying past.

HOLY SPIRIT

*The Holy Spirit
Comes softly,
Gentle like the wind.
Jacob felt Him
In his heart
Changing him within.*

KING SAUL

Old King Saul
Was a grumpy old soul
When he did not
Get his way.

He called for David
To play his harp
And it chased
His grumpies away.

BASKET BOAT

Tweedy, reedy, weedy,
Little basket boat;
Hear the baby crying
As it gently floats.

Comes a princess beautiful
Finds the baby there;
Picks him up,
Gives him back,
For mother's gentle care.

JEHOSHAPHAT

Jehoshaphat, Jehoshaphat,
Marching for the Lord.
God said,
"The war is not yours to fight,
So put away your sword."

GOD'S HOME

Solomon built
A home for God
So He could live
With man.

God wanted to
Be with us
So we could
Understand,

How much He
Truly loves us
And to give us
A helping hand.

BUILDING A TEMPLE

Jingle, jangle, jingle
In the money chest,
Coins to build a temple,
Made only of the best.

Working, saving, giving,
Will you now invest?
Give you coins to Jesus
Do your very best?

Ringing, singing, praising,
On this day of rest,
Come into the temple
There you will be blest.

MARY, MARY

Mary, Mary
Quite contrary
How your money goes
To buy perfume
In a pretty box
To put upon some toes.

Mary, Mary
Quiet and meek
Washing Jesus' feet
With rich perfume,
Your long black hair
And tears of love so sweet.

THE LION'S DEN

The lion's den
Is dark and cool.
See how the lions
Slobber and drool.

As Daniel sits
Upon the ground
Angels gather
All around.

Angels guard
And safely keep
While lions pace
And Daniel sleeps.

PETER GOES FREE

Prison doors
Swing open wide
At the angel's touch.

Peter's chains
Fall to his side.
"Thank you, angel,
Very much."

EUTYCHUS

Eutychus, Eutychus
Sat on a window sill.
Eutychus, Eutychus
Had a great spill.
All the king's horses
And all the king's men
Couldn't bring Eutychus
To life again.

Paul who was preaching
Came down to see
Eutychus lying
As still as could be.

Paul bent down and
Touched the boy.
Eutychus got up
Shouting for joy.

LOST AND FOUND

A sheep in the meadow
Lost his way,
Wandering around
In the hills all day.

The Shepherd went out
And found his sheep.
"Baa, Baa, Baa," came
From the canyon deep.

He picked up the sheep
From the canyon floor,
Carried it home
To wander no more.

BLACK SHEEP

Baa Baa
Black sheep
Running from the Lord.
STOP,
Rest a while,
Think upon His word.

Baa Baa
Black sheep
Coming to the Lord,
GET UP
From your rest,
Take the gospel sword.

Baa Baa
Black sheep
Witness for the Lord,
GO NOW,
Tell all the world
About the love of God.

JESUS AND LUCIFER

Lucifer,
Son of the Morning,
Falling from heaven's grace,
Now you must leave
The Father,
Live in another place.

Lucifer,
Son of the Morning,
Fallen in your disgrace,
Now you will wander
My world
Tempting the human race.

Jesus,
The Son of Yahweh,
Lovingly comes to save,
All who come to
Know Him
And look upon His face.

Jesus,
The Son of Yahweh,
Here from the Father's throne,
Strengthens His own
Dear children
To run the Christian race.

THREE ANGELS

Three angels' voices
Sound the alarm.
Listen to each,
They'll keep you from harm.

The first angel comes
With the gospel to tell.
Worship God the creator
So He judges you well.

The second angel comes.
He wants us to tell
Truth over falsehood
And know it quite well.

The third angel comes
To prevent our surprise
And tells us the mark
Of the image that lies.

The beast wants the worship
Belonging to God,
And changes God's law
With a wink and a nod.

Tradition means more
To the ones who won't hear
The three angels' voices
With warnings so clear.

Take heed who you worship
For the true God above
Is longing to give us
His message of love.

BIBLE TEXTS & THOUGHTS FOR PARENTS

Ask, and it shall be given you;

Seek, and you shall find;

Knock, and it shall be opened unto you:

For everyone that asks receives;

And he that seeks finds;

To him that knocks it shall be opened.

(paraphrase of Matthew 7:7, 8)

God assures us that we will receive all His promises and blessings as we ask and seek for them. The following are thoughts that you as the parent can expand as you read and discuss the poems with your child. The Bible texts are here for you to read the story from the Bible. All texts have been taken from the King James edition of the Bible, but other translations can be read as well.

GOD'S LETTER — Exodus 20:1–17; Jeremiah 31:31–33

The Ten Commandments were given by God as a rule of life. The first four teach us how to worship the true Creator God and the last six tell us how to treat each other. Through Christ's death and the work of the Holy Spirit, His laws are written in our hearts.

Prayer thought: Ask God to help you be the kind of person spoken about in the Commandments.

LIGHT YOUR CANDLE — Matthew 5:14–16; John 3:19–21

We are known by our actions and whether they are witnesses for God. When we let the Holy Spirit change our lives, everyone we meet will know. Our life will be like a shining candle in the world, no matter where we go. God will know us by the life we live.

Prayer thought: Ask God to help you act in such a way that He will recognize you as His child when He looks down from heaven.

EDEN LOST — Genesis 3

Adam, the first man, created by God, lost his leadership over the new world God created. He thought knowing evil would make him as wise as God and was not satisfied with the boundaries God had given him. He believed the lie of the serpent in the garden rather than believing what God told him. With his wife, Eve, he had to leave the beautiful garden that God had made for their home. God made a promise to Adam and Eve that He would eventually defeat the serpent. Until that time the people on the earth would have to live with the effects of their choice.

Prayer thought: Ask God to show you the right choices to make today.

THE ARK — Genesis 7:1–24

God gave Noah instructions to build the ark. It was for protection from the worldwide flood that was to come on the world. It took Noah 120 years to build the ark. The people saw him building the ark and laughed at him. They had a long time to make the decision to believe God and prepare for the flood. Noah, his wife, three sons, and their wives were the only ones who believed God and were saved in the ark. The others were lost because they didn't believe God.

Prayer thought: Thank God for helping you believe Him and His word and to follow His directions.

HOLY SPIRIT — John 3:5–8

We cannot see the Holy Spirit. We can only see and feel how He changes our lives. He brings good thoughts to our mind and the desire to be a better person. He will change your heart when you ask Him to change it. You know the Holy Spirit is working in your heart when your thoughts and actions change for the better.

Prayer thought: Every day ask for the Holy Spirit to help you be willing for Him to change your heart to follow His leading. Ask for help to be loving and kind.

BIBLE TEXTS & THOUGHTS FOR PARENTS

JACOB'S LIE — Genesis 28:10–15, 41–44; Genesis 32:24–30

God loves us even when we lie, cheat, steal, and break His commandments. When we are truly sorry for doing those things and allow the Holy Spirit to change us, God forgives us. His promise of protection goes with us wherever we go. Jacob allowed the Holy Spirit to change his heart to be sorry for cheating his brother and to help him live a truthful life.

Prayer thought: Ask God to help you to be truthful, kind, and loving today. Thank Him for keeping you safe while you play.

KING SAUL — 1 Samuel 9:1, 2, 15–19, 25–27; 10:1; 16:14–23

The Israelites wanted a king so they could be like the surrounding nations. God chose Saul. He looked like a king. He was handsome and stood head and shoulders taller than the average man. However, his character was not kingly. He was moody and did not follow God's directions in leading Israel. He chose to follow his own ways. Though physically he was a grown man, his character was that of a selfish child. He had an evil spirit that came upon him. David was able to soothe the king by playing his harp.

Prayer thought: When you become angry today, ask God to chase the anger away and give you peace.

BASKET BOAT — Exodus 2:1–10

Moses was protected by God through the actions of his parents. God had a plan for Moses' life. He would someday lead the children of Israel out of Egypt and into the Promised Land. God has a plan for your life.

Prayer thought: Ask God to show you what His plan is for you and allow God to lead you. Thank Him for showing you His plan.

JEHOSHAPHAT — 2 Chronicles 20:5–30

There were three armies coming to war against Judah. Jehoshaphat came to God asking Him to protect them. God sent word through His prophet that He would fight the battle. The men of Judah were instructed to go out and stand and see what the Lord would do for them. They were not to be discouraged or afraid. God would be with them as they faced their enemies. The armies started fighting among themselves and God's people didn't have to fight at all.

Prayer thought: Ask God to help you let Him fight your battles today. Let Him show you what He will do for you. Thank Him for fighting your battles.

GOD'S HOME — 1 Kings 8:6–11; 8:23–30

God wants a relationship with us. The first permanent temple was built by Solomon. God wanted to be with His people. His presence was in the cloud that sat over the mercy seat in the Most Holy Place. We cannot see God because of sin. Knowing His presence was there comforted the people. They came there to pray, to ask for forgiveness, and to get help from God.

Prayer thought: When you go to church think about the church being God's house. Pray that you will be reverent. Thank God for having a church where you can go and learn more about Him.

WIDOW'S MITE — Mark 12:42–44; Luke 21:1–4

Jesus saw a widow quietly putting a very small amount of money into the offering box. It was all the money she had. Other people who had a lot of money were only giving a small amount but were making a big show of how much they were giving. Jesus wants us to give to Him with a willing heart because we love Him—not as a show for other people to see and give us praise. He will bless what we give willingly to Him.

Prayer thought: Ask God to show you what you can give to help others today. It doesn't have to be a lot. He can bless even a penny.

BIBLE TEXTS & THOUGHTS FOR PARENTS

BUILDING A TEMPLE — 2 Chronicles 24:1–14

Joash was seven-years-old when he became king over Judah. As a teenager he wanted to repair the Temple in Jerusalem. He set up a chest at the entrance of the Temple, where the people happily brought their offerings. The Temple was restored and everyone who came to worship there was blessed.

Prayer thought: God will bless whatever you can do for Him, even if you are very small and don't think you have a lot to give. Thank God for your blessings and that you can share them with others.

MARY, MARY — Luke 7:36–38

Mary was very thankful for Jesus' forgiveness of her sins. To show her thankfulness she spent her money on some very expensive perfume to wash Jesus' feet. What can you do to show Jesus how thankful you are for what he has done for you?

Prayer thought: Thank God for forgiving you when you have done wrong and for helping you to do better.

THE LION'S DEN — Daniel 6

Daniel was faithful to God even when he might be killed. His relationship with God was more important than his life. God saved him from the hungry lions. It showed the King, who respected Daniel, that God was able to take care of His own.

Prayer thought: Ask God to make you brave when you stand up for Him. Be faithful and He will take care of you. Thank God for the strength He gives you to stand up for Him.

PETER GOES FREE — Acts 12: 6–10

Peter was thankful for what the angel did for him. We can be thankful for what God does for us every day also. We should always tell God thank you in our prayers.

Prayer thought: Thank God for making you free from wrong thoughts and habits.

EUTYCHUS — Acts 20:6–12

Paul had been speaking and preaching all day. A young boy sitting in a third story window fell asleep while listening to Paul preach. Eutychus didn't do anything wrong when he fell asleep. It is hard for young children to sit still for so long listening to grown-ups talk. Sitting for a long time makes people sleepy. When Eutychus fell out of the window, he died. God brought him back to life through Paul. Sometimes accidents happen to us when we are not careful.

Prayer thought: Ask God to help you to be careful while you are playing.

LOST AND FOUND — Luke 15:3–7

The sheep wandered so far away from the flock while eating and looking for better grass that he became separated before he realized it. He wandered around looking for the shepherd and the flock he belonged to. The shepherd realized he was missing a sheep, so he went out and found him. He was so happy to find him that he carried the sheep home and had a party. God wants you to stay with His people. We are always looking for something better in this life to make us happy, but it can take us away from God and His protection and care. Things like cars, homes, money, and toys can sometimes become more important in our lives than our relationship with God.

Prayer thought: Ask God to make Him the most important person in your life.

BLACK SHEEP — Matthew 28:18–20

A family member who chooses to do wrong things and get into crime is often referred to as the "black sheep" of the family. God can change their hearts if they are willing for Him to do so and become great witnesses of the power of God. You can tell others about how much God loves you and wants you to do what is right.

Prayer thought: Ask God to help you be a witness to someone and tell them that God loves them.

BIBLE TEXTS & THOUGHTS FOR PARENTS

JESUS AND LUCIFER — Revelation 12:7–11; Isaiah 14:12–14

Lucifer wanted to be like God and did not want to follow God's instructions. He fought God in heaven. Because of that Lucifer could no longer live there. He was sent to the earth to live. Now Lucifer is trying to convince the people on earth to live the way they want to and not obey God's instructions. Jesus came to earth to save us from Satan's lies. God created us; He is the only one who can give us life.

Prayer thought: Thank God every day for the life He gives you.

THREE ANGELS — Revelation 14:6–11

This is God's last warning message to the world before He comes to end sin on this earth. It is a message about worshiping the true God, the One who created everything. God wants us to know His Word well enough so that we can tell what is true and what is false. God's law was written for humanity to obey. There are those who think they can change God's law and do what they want to. These people who think they can change God's law will try to convince the world that they have the authority to do so. It is very important to know God and what He has said in His Word, the Bible, so you will not follow the traditions of this world.

Prayer thought: Ask God every day to show you what truth is and how to live the truth in your life so He will recognize you as His child when He comes back.

We invite you to view the complete
selection of titles we publish at:

www.TEACHServices.com

scan with your mobile
device to go directly
to our website

Please write or email us your praises, reactions, or
thoughts about this or any other book we publish at:

11 Quartermaster Circle
Fort Oglethorpe, GA 30742

Info@TEACHServices.com

TEACH Services, Inc., titles may be purchased in bulk for
educational, business, fund-raising, or sales promotional use.
For information, please e-mail:

BulkSales@TEACHServices.com

Finally if you are interested in seeing
your own book in print, please contact us at

publishing@TEACHServices.com

We would be happy to review your manuscript for free.

www.ingramcontent.com/pod-product-compliance
Lightning Source LLC
Chambersburg PA
CBHW061118170426
43199CB00026B/2959